Full-Speed Sports

The Science of a Triple Axel

Ellen Labrecque

Published in the United States of America by Cherry Lake Publishing
Ann Arbor, Michigan
www.cherrylakepublishing.com

Content Adviser: Dr. Thomas Carroll, Associate Professor of Physics and Astronomy, Ursinus College
Reading Adviser: Marla Conn, ReadAbility, Inc.

Photo Credits: © technotr/iStock.com, cover, 1; © Iurii Osadchi/Shutterstock.com, 5, 6, 16, 18, 19, 22; © Beryl Peters Collection/Alamy, 9; ©AlexAranda/Shutterstock.com, 10 ; Paul Kitagaki Jr./ZUMApress/Newscom, 13; © Vkovalcik | Dreamstime.com - Tilted Natural Version, Ice Skates Photo, 15; © Jeremy Nicholl/Alamy, 21; © Tribune Content Agency LLC/Alamy, 25; © Digitalexpressionimages | Dreamstime.com - Zamboni Preps The Ice Photo, 26; © Olga Besnard/ Shutterstock.com, 25

Library of Congress Cataloging-in-Publication Data

Labrecque, Ellen.
 The science of a triple axel/Ellen Labrecque.
 pages cm.—(Full-Speed Sports)
Includes index.
Audience: Age: 8–12.
Audience: Grade: 4 to 6.
 ISBN 978-1-63362-587-7 (hardcover)—ISBN 978-1-63362-767-3 (pdf)—ISBN 978-1-63362-677-5 (paperback)—
ISBN 978-1-63362-857-1 (ebook)
 1. Figure skating—Juvenile literature. I. Title.

 GV850.4.L33 2015
 796.91'2—dc23
                    2014050352

Cherry Lake Publishing would like to acknowledge the work of
the Partnership for 21st Century Skills. Please visit *www.p21.org*
for more information.

Printed in the United States of America
Corporate Graphics

ABOUT THE AUTHOR

Ellen Labrecque is a freelance writer living in Pennsylvania with her husband and two kids. She has written many non-fiction books and previously was an editor at *Sports Illustrated Kids* magazine. An avid runner, Ellen is always trying to figure out ways to become speedier.

TABLE OF CONTENTS

CHAPTER 1

An Amazing Competitor

It is the Winter Olympics in Sochi, Russia, in February 2014. Figure skater Yuzuru Hanyu of Japan, age 19, is competing in his first Olympics.

About halfway through his program, Hanyu attempts one of skating's hardest jumps, the triple axel. He skates forward at 12 miles (19 kilometers) per hour. His arms and right leg are out. He bends his left leg and swings his arms back. As he launches off his left outside skate edge, his arms are waist-high as he begins to lift. Hanyu rises into the air and rotates 3.5 times around. As he

[21ST CENTURY SKILLS LIBRARY]

The last part of a triple axel involves skating backward, which Yuzuru Hanyu nailed in the 2014 Winter Olympics.

Hanyu won a gold medal in the 2014 Winter Olympics.

spins, he keeps his arms tightly tucked into his body and his legs twisted together. He lands cleanly on his right skate and begins to skate backward. The crowd erupts in cheers. The judges' scores reward his great technique. Hanyu becomes the first skater to break the 100-point mark in the short-skate competition. After the long-skate competition one day later, he wins his first Olympic gold medal.

How did Hanyu skate so beautifully and make it look so easy? How did he execute the triple axel so flawlessly? Simply put, it's the science behind his skating!

THINK ABOUT IT

The triple axel is the only jump in figure skating that requires the skater to take off from a forward motion instead of a backward motion. All jumps, though, end with the skater landing backward. This means to complete a triple axel, a skater has to go around 3.5 times instead of just three. Which other parts of the triple axel sound difficult to you?

CHAPTER 2

HOW SKATING STARTED

Ice skating began a long time ago. Scientists found a skate at the bottom of a lake in Switzerland and determined it was from 3000 BCE. These first skates were made from the leg bones of large animals such as horses, deer, or elk. These early European skaters weren't skating for fun, but instead to get around on frozen rivers and lakes during the long winter months.

Skating spread around the world in the 1700s and 1800s. The British discovered that skating didn't just have to be useful; it could also be fun. They came up with the

Skating became a popular pastime in England in the 1800s.

idea of carving forms, such as circles and figure eights, into the ice with their skates. This is how the sport of figure skating got its name. In early figure skating competitions, there was no jumping at all. Instead, competitors were judged on how well they made etchings in the ice with their blades.

American Jackson Haines introduced jumps into the skating world in the mid-1800s. He studied music and dance as a boy and thought skating could be combined with dancing.

Mao Asada is a well-known skater from Japan.

Figure skating was the first winter sport to be part of the Olympic Games, in 1908. Jumps were included, but actual "figure" skating—or tracing patterns—remained the most important part of the competition.

This all changed when television first broadcast the Winter Olympic Games in 1956. Audiences found the figure tracing part of the sport boring, but they loved to watch skaters jump and spin. The 1992 Winter Olympics eliminated figure tracing from the competition all together. Instead, there was a short program and a long program that both included skaters executing a number of jumps and spins. The bigger and higher the jumps, the higher the scores and louder the cheers.

The axel jump is named for Norwegian skater Axel Paulsen, who first did a single axel jump (1.5 times around) in the late 1800s. U.S. figure skater Dick Button performed the first double axel in competition at the 1948 Olympics. But no skater was able to do the triple axel until 30 years later. Canadian Vern Taylor performed the first triple axel at the 1978 World Figure Skating Championships.

THINK ABOUT IT!

In order to complete a triple axel, skaters need strength and power to get the height they need to complete 3.5 rotations. What muscles need to be strong to perform a triple axel?

Midori Ito of Japan was the first woman to perform a triple axel in competition. She accomplished this feat in 1988, a decade after Taylor's first triple axel. Since then, only four other women figure skaters have landed the triple axel jump in an international competition. At the 2010 Winter Olympics in Vancouver, Canada, Mao Asada of Japan landed three triple axels! Mistakes in her routine, however, kept her from winning the gold medal. She went home with the silver.

In the 2010 Winter Olympics, Mao Asada landed three triple axels.

— CHAPTER 3 —

SUPER SKATING SCIENCE

Thanks to advancements in training, as well as in science and technology, figure skaters fly higher and make more difficult jumps than ever before.

"A figure skating jump is a complicated skill that combines a lot of different motions in it," says Deborah King, a professor of sports science at Ithaca College and an advisor to United States Figure Skating.

When a figure skater attempts a triple axel, he or she must gain a lot of speed before lifting off for the jump. **Friction** plays two roles here. At first, the skater needs

Smooth ice helps the skater move faster.
Scratched ice slows the skater down.

enough **traction** between the skates and the ice to push off and generate speed. Yet, the smooth ice provides a low level of resistance against the skate's blades, allowing the skater to glide along the ice and stay in motion after pushing off. The skater moves his or her feet to change the angles at which the blades touch the ice.

Skaters use this speed to create lift. They don't stop when they get ready to jump, but instead allow their **momentum** to help them soar high into the air.

After being thrown by her partner, Felicia Zhang holds her arms tight to her body to spin faster.

When skaters prepare to take off into the air, they use their leg muscles to push off the ice. A scientific law is at work here: For every action, there is an equal and opposite reaction. So when the skater pushes off (the action), the ice acts like a **force** that pushes back (the reaction). The harder the skater pushes off, the higher he flies in the air.

Once in the air, the skater's body becomes a projectile. A projectile is an object that moves with **gravity** as the only noticeable outside force acting on it. The skater's speed parallel to the ground stays the same. But, the skater's velocity is changing: the vertical component of speed he gained on takeoff gets smaller and smaller. Gravity is acting on the skater the entire time he is in the air, eventually pulling him back down to the ice.

When a skater attempts the triple axel, he is following a law of motion called the **conservation of angular momentum**. (Anything that has **mass** and velocity also has momentum. If the velocity is in a circular direction, it's called angular momentum.) This law says that you can't just "lose" momentum—it has to go somewhere.

Michael Christian Martinez was the first-ever ice skater from the Philippines to qualify for the Olympics.

LOOK!

Look at how tightly this figure skater keeps his body as he spins high into the air. What would happen if he spread his arms wide? Would his spinning speed up or slow down?

Peter Liebers, from Germany, fell during the 2014 Winter Olympics.

Angular momentum is the combination of how big something is and how fast it's spinning. So if the figure skater were big with his arms extended, his momentum would go into the act of him reaching his arms out. But, if he makes himself smaller by pulling his arms in, the momentum would go into spinning him faster. This is the most effective way to perform a triple axel.

A skater lands a triple axel backwards and in a position where he can maintain his balance. He doesn't want to land standing straight up, but instead land leaning slightly forward and crouched. This position minimizes the impact on the skater's legs and allows him to slow down more easily.

CHAPTER 4

THE ICE SKATING IMPACT

Thanks to the added thrills (and sometimes spills) of the jumps, figure skating is one of the most popular sports at the Winter Olympics. And although figure skaters make it look effortless as they nail jumps like the triple axel, landing these jumps take a lot of practice. Skaters train up to five days a week all year long, performing 50 to 100 jumps per session. This is a lot of strain on a body! The landing force from a triple axel equals eight to 10 times the skater's body weight. This means when a 100-pound skater lands a triple axel, her

A coach helps a skater learn better form.

legs absorb the **impact** of up to 1,000 pounds! To understand this idea, think about a car that is traveling at a high speed. If this fast car hits a brick wall, it will really damage the car. But if the car is moving at a much slower speed, it won't be as damaged when it hits the wall. The figure skater doing the triple axel is like the fast-moving car! When the skater hits the ice, the impact is hard!

As a result, skaters often suffer stress fractures in their legs and spines. Olympic champion Tara Lipinski needed hip surgery when she was only 18 years old.

Sometimes falls can badly injure skaters. Luckily, Jeremy Abbott was able to get up and finish his program.

[21ST CENTURY SKILLS LIBRARY]

Russian figure skating star Evgeni Plushenko had to drop out of the 2014 Olympics because of his bad back. Prior to the Games, he had already had 12 back surgeries.

Although nobody has nailed it in a competition or practice, skaters are now on a quest to do a quadruple axel, which is 4.5 times around. As skaters push themselves harder the safety and the health of these athletes has to be a top priority.

"We always have to be thinking about risk versus reward when skaters are attempting the next big jump," explains Mitch Moyer, Senior Director of Athlete High Performance with U.S. Figure Skating.

GO DEEPER!

Reread this chapter closely. Knowing all the concerns about injuries, do you think figure skating is a dangerous sport? Why or why not? Can you think of other sports in which athletes might have similar injuries?

CHAPTER 5

SKATING INTO THE FUTURE

Researchers and scientists are coming up with new training methods that make skating more exciting but also safer. Modern science technologies, such as motion capture imaging and special blades, are helping this cause.

Motion capturing is a video technology that's able to recognize where every point on a person's body is during movement. Before heading out on the ice, skaters put special reflective stickers all over themselves. Computer sensors pick up on these stickers and show an outline of the skater's body during a jump. Coaches and scientists can then change the body position, such as moving an arm up or down, on the computer screen, to see what would make the jump better. This kind of information teaches athletes how to get the increased spin or the higher lift needed to perform the trick they are trying to master.

Biomechanic students at the University of Delaware applied reflective dots to this figure skater to measure her movement.

Zambonis smooth out the scratches that skates leave on the ice.

Scientists have also created "smart" ice-skating blades. The blades measure the force of the impact when skaters land a jump. Based on the results, these blades could inspire new training ideas for skaters, such as limiting jumps per practice or encouraging more training off the ice.

Skaters now use harnesses when practicing, which were popularized by skating coach Nick Perna around 2001. The harness goes around the skater's body and is attached to fishing pole-like device that the coach holds while standing nearby. When a skater begins to fall, the

GO DEEPER

The Zamboni is a brand of ice resurfacing machine invented in 1949. It used to be that to get smooth ice, someone had to shave it and then water it by hand. The Zamboni, which looks like a ride-on tractor, simply drives over the ice, making it smoother than it was before. Reread chapter 3. How do you think this affects the friction on a skater's blades? What do you think are the pros and cons to skating on fresh ice?

Chang Peng and Hao Zhang, from China,
performed this "death spiral" in Paris in 2012.

rope system pulls the skater back up and prevents him from hitting the ice. This takes the stress off skaters' hips, knees, and backs as they learn the triple axel and other challenging jumps.

Figure skating has become one of the most athletic sports out there, but what can be done next? How much higher or how many more spins can skaters safely do in the near future? Nobody knows for sure. But no matter how much higher, bigger, or faster they go, science is sure to play a role in skating's next frontier!

[21ST CENTURY SKILLS LIBRARY]

TIMELINE

A TIMELINE HISTORY OF FIGURE SKATING

3000 BCE	People make the first skates using animal bones.
1700 CE	The sport of figure skating is born.
1882	Norwegian skater Axel Paulsen does the first axel jump (a single jump, 1.5 times around).
1908	Figure skating makes its debut at the Olympics in London, England.
1948	U.S. figure skater Dick Button performs the first double axel in competition at the Olympics in St. Moritz, Switzerland.
1956	The Winter Olympics are first broadcast on television in Europe.
1961	The entire U.S. figure skating team, including their coaches, is killed in a plane crash in Belgium, on their way to compete in the World Figure Skating Championships.
1978	Vern Taylor performs the first triple axel at the 1978 World Figure Skating Championships.
1987	Brian Orser of Canada is the first skater to put two triple axel jumps in the same program; he is also the first skater to land three triple axel jumps in the same competition.
1988	Midori Ito of Japan is the first woman to land the triple axel jump in competition.
1991	Tonya Harding of the United States is the first woman to land two triple axels in the same competition.
2010	Mao Asada is the first woman to land three triple axels in the same competition at the Winter Olympics in Vancouver, Canada.

THINK ABOUT IT

Think about what you knew about the triple axel and figure skating before reading this book. Does the jump seem harder or easier to do now that you have been introduced to some of the science behind it?

In chapter 3, you learned about the law of science called the conservation of angular momentum. This law suggests that the more open the skater's body, the slower the skater spins. The tighter the skater's body, the faster the skater spins! Do you think you could show how this works on your own? How could you do it?

Do you think skaters should keep performing triple axels? Why or why not? Make a list of pros and cons.

If figure skating had fewer jumps, do you think fans would keep watching the sport? Why or why not?

[21ST CENTURY SKILLS LIBRARY]

LEARN MORE

FURTHER READING

Challen, Paul. *Spin It Figure Skating*. New York: Crabtree Publishing, 2010.

Thomas, Kelti. *How Figure Skating Works*. Toronto: Maple Tree Press, 2009.

Throp, Claire. *Figure Skating*. Chicago: Raintree, 2014.

WEB SITES

Bleacher Report—US Olympic Figure Skating: Ranking the Top 20 Moments of All Time
http://bleacherreport.com/articles/1922277-us-olympic-figure-skating-ranking-the-top-20-moments-of-all-time
Watch these videos of some amazing figure skating performances.

Scholastic—Ice Skating
www.scholastic.com/teachers/article/ice-skating
Readers can learn about the history of figure skating and how it became the athletic sport it is today.

U.S. Figure Skating
www.usfsa.org
This Web site lets readers stay tuned to all of the news about U.S. Figure Skating.

GLOSSARY

conservation of angular momentum (kahn-sur-VAY-shuhn UHV ANG-gyuh-lur moh-MEN-tuhm) a law of science that states that angular momentum can't disappear, it can only be transferred somewhere else

force (fors) any action that produces, stops, or changes the shape or movement of an object

friction (FRIK-shuhn) a force that results from the rubbing of surfaces against each other

gravity (GRAV-i-tee) the force of attraction pulling any two bodies toward each other; for example, the force of attraction pulling bodies toward the center of the earth

impact (IM-pakt) the forceful striking of one thing against another

mass (mas) the amount of physical matter that an object contains

momentum (moh-MEN-tuhm) the property that a moving object has because of its mass and its motion

traction (TRAK-shuhn) a type of friction that keeps a skater from slipping

INDEX